Allison Lassieur

Crabs,
Lobsters,
and Shrimps

Franklin Watts - A Division of Scholastic Inc.
New York • Toronto • London • Auckland • Sydney
Mexico City • New Delhi • Hong Kong
Danbury, Connecticut

Photographs © 2003: Animals Animals: 31 (Zig Leszczynski), 35 (Fritz Prenzel); Dembinsky Photo Assoc./Jesse Cancelmo: 13; Dr. Tom Iliffet, Texas A&M University at Galveston: 37 (Serban Sarbu); Earth Scenes/Francis Lepine: 41; Natural History Museum, London: 39; Peter Arnold Inc.: 6, 7 (Fred Bavendam), 33 (Jodi Jacobson); Photo Researchers, NY: 5 top right, 5 bottom left (E.R. Degginger), 42 (Jeff Greenberg/MR), cover, 5 top left, 18, 19, 27, 29 (Andrew J. Martinez), 25 (Harry Rogers), 20, 21, 23 (M.H. Sharp); Seapics.com: 15 (Doug Perrine/Innerspace Visions), 1, 5 bottom right (D.R. & T.L. Schrichte); Visuals Unlimited/W.J. Weber: 17.

Illustrations by Pedro Julio Gonzalez, Steve Savage, and A. Natacha Pimentel C.

The photograph on the cover shows a fiddler crab. The photograph on the title page shows two banded coral shrimp.

Library of Congress Cataloging-in-Publication Data

Lassieur, Allison.
    Crabs, lobsters, and shrimps / Allison Lassieur
    p. cm. – (Animals in order)
    Summary: Explores the relationship between members of the decapoda order, including descriptions of several types of lobsters, crabs, and shrimps.
    Includes bibliographical references and index (p.).
    ISBN 0-531-12265-4 (lib. bdg.) 0-531-16659-7 (pbk.)
    1. Decapoda (Crustacea)—Classification—Juvenile literature.
[1. Lobsters. 2. Crabs. 3. Shrimps.] I. Title. II. Series.
QL444.M33L37 2003
595.3'8-dc21
                                                                                2002011293

Contents

A Sea Full of Decapoda

Of all the sea creatures that inhabit the world's waters, decapods are among the most plentiful. Most people have seen decapods before— on restaurant menus! Decapods are commonly known as shellfish in restaurants and grocery stores. People have been consuming decapods for thousands of years. The delicate, sweet flavor of lobsters, shrimps, and crabs makes them valuable foods. In North America, the lobster, shrimp, and crab fishing industries provide these tasty decapods to markets all over the world. People who have never seen an ocean have probably tasted a decapod that once lived there.

Animals in the **order** decapoda have a lot in common with other **crustaceans**, but they're not all the same. Look at the four crustaceans on the next page. Can you tell what they have in common?

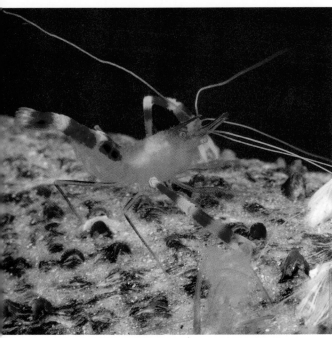
Golden coral shrimp

Hawaiian slipper lobster

Traits of a Decapod

Thousands of species of decapods swim and crawl through the world's oceans. Many of them look alike, but some look very different from one another. Sometimes it's hard to tell that they are even related! But decapods have many traits in common, even though these traits may be hard to see at first glance.

Decapod comes from the Greek *deca*, which means "ten." All decapods have five pairs of legs that are attached to the part of the body called the **thorax**. The first pair of legs usually has large, heavy pincers called **chelipeds**. Decapods use their chelipeds to catch and crush their prey.

Decapods are divided into two main groups: the ones that swim and the ones that crawl. Swimming decapods include shrimps. Shrimps usually have thin, slender bodies. Abdomens, legs, and fan tails all help shrimp to move through the water.

A shrimp is a type of decapod that can swim.

Crabs use their long claws to catch and hold prey.

Lobsters and crabs are crawling decapods. Their bodies are more suited to getting around on foot, with flattened bodies and short, sturdy legs. Their fan tails are usually smaller in proportion to their bodies because they don't need them to swim. Most crawling decapods need large claws for defense and hunting.

Most decapods are what scientists call **predacious**, which means that they will catch and eat any animal that is the right size and is available. Some decapods catch and kill their prey with their claws. Other species of decapod are what scientists call filter feeders. Filter feeders use the fringelike parts of their limbs to catch small pieces of loose, edible material floating in the water.

Decapods live in a variety of **habitats**. Some decapods burrow in the sandy bottoms of rivers and oceans. Others hide in the crevices and cracks of rocks and coral. A few unique kinds of decapods, such as the hermit crab, live in the empty shells of other animals. Some spend the first years of their lives as tiny swimmers and then sink to the bottom to find shelter as they grow older and larger.

The most important role decapods play in the environment is as food for other animals. Newly hatched decapods make up a large part of the plankton that fills the world's oceans. Hundreds of marine species eat plankton. If a decapod survives its plankton stage, it might grow to become food for a larger fish—or a human.

The Order of Living Things

A tiger has more in common with a house cat than it does with a daisy. A decapod is more like a clam than it is like a cougar. Scientists arrange living things into groups based on how they look and act. A tiger and a house cat belong to the same group, but a daisy belongs to a different group.

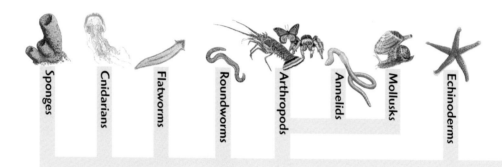

Sponges | Cnidarians | Flatworms | Roundworms | Arthropods | Annelids | Mollusks | Echinoderms

Animals

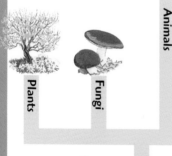

Plants | Fungi

Protists

Monerans

All living things can be placed in one of five groups called **kingdoms**: the plant kingdom, the animal kingdom, the fungus kingdom, the moneran kingdom, or the protist kingdom. You can probably name many of the creatures in the plant and animal kingdoms. The fungus kingdom includes mushrooms, yeasts, and molds. The moneran and protist kingdoms contain thousands of living things that are too small to be seen without a microscope.

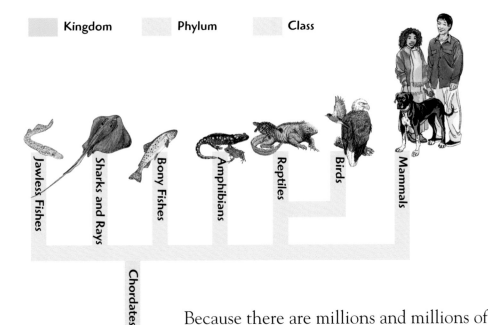

Kingdom   Phylum   Class

Jawless Fishes

Sharks and Rays

Bony Fishes

Amphibians

Reptiles

Birds

Mammals

Chordates

Because there are millions and millions of living things on Earth, some of the members of one kingdom may not seem all that similar. The animal kingdom includes creatures as different as tarantulas and trout, jellyfishes and jaguars, salamanders and sparrows, elephants and earthworms.

To show that an elephant is more like a jaguar than it is like an earthworm, scientists further separate the creatures in each kingdom into smaller groups. The animal kingdom can be divided into nine phyla. Humans belong to the chordate phylum. All chordates have backbones.

Each phylum is subdivided into many **classes**. Humans, mice, and elephants all belong to the mammal class. Each class can be further divided into orders; orders into **families**, families into **genera**, and genera into **species**. All of the members of a species are very similar.

9

How Decapods Fit In

You can probably guess that decapods belong to the animal kingdom. They have more in common with snakes and spiders than they do with maple trees and morning glories.

Decapods belong to the arthropod phylum. All arthropods have tough outer skins. Can you guess what other living things might be arthropods? Examples include true bugs, spiders, mites, ticks, millipedes, and centipedes.

The arthropod phylum can be divided into a number of classes. Decapods belong to the crustacea class.

Decapods can be divided into a number of different families and genera. There are more than eight thousand different species of decapods in the world. They can be found in freshwater and saltwater throughout the world, but they are most abundant in the Atlantic Ocean. In this book, you will learn about fourteen different species of decapods.

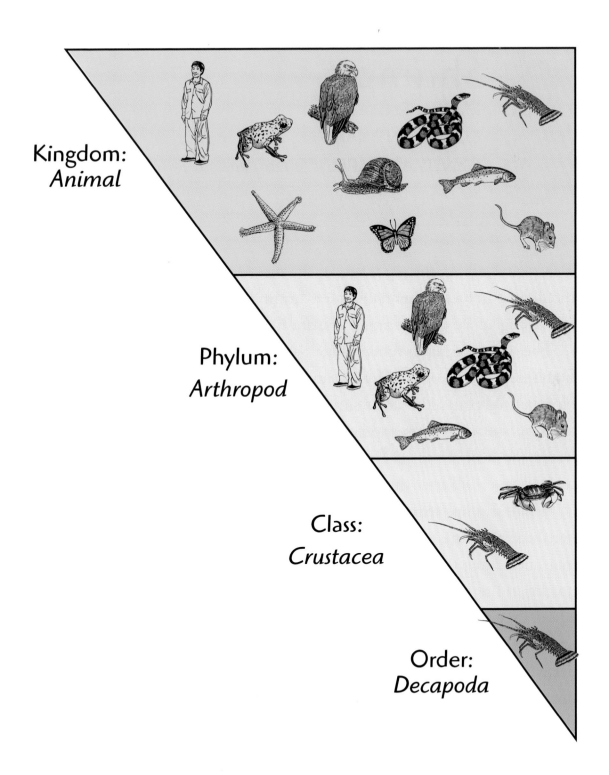

Kingdom:
Animal

Phylum:
Arthropod

Class:
Crustacea

Order:
Decapoda

Shrimps

FAMILY: Penaeidae
COMMON EXAMPLE: White shrimp
GENUS AND SPECIES: *Litopenaeus setiferus*
SIZE: up to 10 inches (25 centimeters)

This plain-looking shrimp is one of the most important members of the decapod order. When you order shrimp in a restaurant or buy it by the bag at the grocery store, you are likely to get white shrimps.

The white shrimp is found along the east coast of the United States from New York to Florida, and in the Gulf of Mexico from Florida to Mexico. But white shrimps' favorite places are marshy areas in South Carolina and Louisiana. Shrimp boats travel these waters for most of the year, catching tons of these shrimps to satisfy seafood lovers all over the country.

White shrimps **spawn** by the millions from May to August. Fertilized eggs sink to the bottom of the ocean, and twelve to twenty-four hours later, they hatch into tiny **larvae**. These larvae grow quickly, riding the tides into the marshes, **estuaries**, and tidal creeks, where they are safe from predators. They hide in the dense vegetation and eat almost everything they find, including worms, plant matter, decaying animals, and even other shrimps! These nursery habitats nurture the growing shrimps until they are big enough to return to the ocean to spawn.

Shrimps
FAMILY: Stenopodidae
COMMON EXAMPLE: Banded coral shrimp
GENUS AND SPECIES: *Stenopus hispidus*
SIZE: 2 1/2 inches (6 cm)

This small shrimp is so colorful that it has acquired many names: banded coral shrimp, bandanna shrimp, and even barber-pole shrimp. Other members of this family are sometimes called boxing shrimps because they hold their pincers like boxers ready to fight.

Banded coral shrimps are commonly found in warmer water near coral reefs, rocks, and shipwrecks. They usually hang upside down in caves or crevices. Their habitat ranges from the western Atlantic Ocean down to Florida, Brazil, South Africa, Hawaii, Japan, and Australia.

Unlike other shrimps, banded coral shrimps form mating pairs when they are juveniles and may stay together for years. Most of the time, the female in the pair is much larger than her male mate. Sometimes the male enjoys a ride on the female's back.

Banded coral shrimps feed on **parasites** and matter on the bodies of other fishes and eels. They crawl all over a much larger fish, using their pincers to pick off tiny specs of food they find. In some cases, groups of shrimps form "cleaning stations" on a coral reef. Larger fishes visit these stations looking for a cleaning, so several shrimps climb onto a fish to get a ride and a meal.

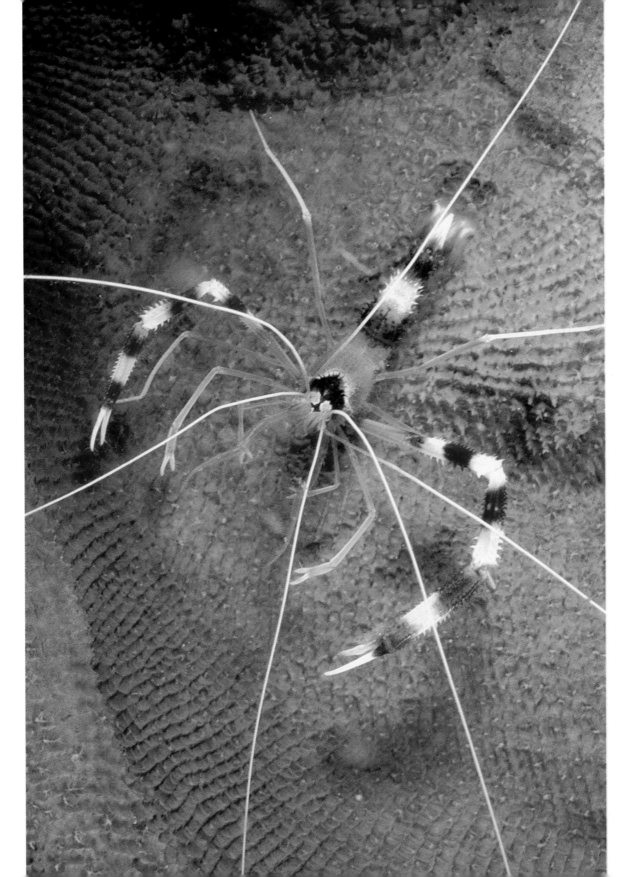

Shrimps

FAMILY: Palaemonidae

COMMON EXAMPLE: California freshwater shrimp

GENUS AND SPECIES: *Syncaris pacifica*

SIZE: 2 1/2 inches (5 cm)

The California freshwater shrimp is one shrimp species that doesn't live in the oceans. Instead, these small, ghostly shrimps can be found only in a few of California's freshwater streams.

These shrimps are different from other shrimp species in that they are terrible swimmers. They cling to the tangled roots and grasses alongside quiet, tree-lined banks. The shrimps find food by grabbing tiny pieces of organic matter that float by.

Most of these shrimps appear clear, with a few colored spots scattered on their bodies. The coloring makes them look like underwater roots. Some shrimps have darker coloring so they can blend in with underwater shadows. This makes them invisible to **predators** such as fishes.

These shrimps are found only in about fifteen California streams. Today, many of those streams are in danger of being destroyed. Pollution is a big problem. Also, many small streams are being rebuilt with concrete sides. This destroys the rough, tree-lined banks that the shrimps need to survive. But scientists are hopeful that the species will survive.

Lobsters

FAMILY: Nephropidae
COMMON EXAMPLE: American lobster
GENUS AND SPECIES: *Homarus americanus*
SIZE: 2 feet (61 cm)

The American lobster is probably the most famous and most studied of the North American decapods. Lobster is considered a luxury food by most people.

American lobsters can be found in the waters off the coast of Canada all the way down to North Carolina, but they are most abundant in Maine. That's why this species is also known as the Maine lobster. The American lobster has huge front chelipeds, or pincers. One pincer is usually larger than the other. The big one is the crushing claw, and the smaller one is the biting claw. Lobster fishermen and scientists can tell if a lobster is "right clawed" or "left clawed" by the size of its chelipeds. The bigger the claw, the more often that lobster uses it to hunt and fight.

Female lobsters lay thousands of eggs about once every two years. Newly hatched lobsters don't look anything like lobsters. In fact, lobstermen call the tiny larvae "lobster bugs." If a lobster bug survives, it will **molt** three times before it starts looking like a lobster. Then it will search for a good hiding place on the ocean floor. The lobster will stay

18

in its hidden home for years, until it is large enough to venture out without being eaten.

Lobsters hunt their prey at night, crawling along the ocean floor looking for crabs, clams, snails, fishes, and even other lobsters for a meal. Sometimes they will catch a crab, drag it home, and bury it like a dog buries a bone. Then, instead of hunting, the lobster will dine on the crab until it is gone.

Crabs

FAMILY: Diogenidae
COMMON EXAMPLE: Striped hermit crab
GENUS AND SPECIES: *Clibanarius vittatus*
SIZE: 1 1/4 to 3 inches (3 to 6 cm)

A crab's entire body usually is covered with a hard shell. But not the hermit crab. This decapod does not have any protection on its abdomen, so it uses the discarded shells of other creatures to protect itself. It slides into a shell and uses special limbs to hold onto the inside of its new home. Then the crab drags the shell along wherever it goes.

The hermit crab's abdomen is bent so that it will fit inside the shell. The crab also has small appendages that it uses to hang onto the shell from the inside. If the hermit crab senses danger, it squeezes deeply into its shell and uses its pincers to guard the entrance.

As the hermit crab grows, it gets too big for its shell and has to find a larger one. This is a dangerous time. As it crawls from one shell to the other, it is open to attack from a predator. But once it is inside its new shell, it will be safer and will have plenty of room to grow.

Sometimes a hermit crab will let other animals, such as sponges or sea anemones, attach themselves to its shell. They help protect the crab and give it excellent camouflage from predators. When the crab moves into a new shell, it might even clip its houseguests off the old shell and transplant them onto the new one.

Crabs

FAMILY: Portunidae
COMMON EXAMPLE: Blue crab
GENUS AND SPECIES: *Callinectes sapidus*
SIZE: about 8 inches (20 cm)

The blue crab's scientific name means "beautiful savory swimmer." It is derived from Latin and Greek words *calli* (beautiful), *nectes* (swimmer), and *sapidus* (savory, or sharp-tasting). Its common name comes from its vibrant blue claws and its blue-green shell.

This decapod is a strong swimmer, using its two back legs as powerful paddles to hurl itself through the water. On land, it scampers along the sand sideways on its three middle pairs of legs. That way, its front pincers are free and ready for fighting or for grabbing some food. A blue crab will eat fish, worms, plants, and just about anything smaller than itself—including other blue crabs.

Sometimes blue crabs are called "soft-shell" crabs, but they do not have soft shells all the time. The soft-shell phase occurs right after a crab molts. For a few days the crab's new shell is soft, which makes it more vulnerable to predators. One blue crab might molt into the soft-shell phase up to twenty-five times during its lifetime.

Blue crabs can be found from Nova Scotia, Canada, all the way to Argentina, South America, but they are most common in the Chesapeake Bay area of the United States. Maryland is known for its blue crab industry. People travel to Maryland from around the world to sample tasty soft-shell crabs and crab cakes served in local restaurants. Blue crab is so popular in Maryland that the state has voted the blue crab as its official state crustacean.

Crabs

FAMILY: Ocypodidae
COMMON EXAMPLE: Atlantic marsh fiddler crab
GENUS AND SPECIES: *Uca pugnax*
SIZE: about 1/2 inch to 1 1/2 inches (1 to 3 cm)

If you walk through a marsh mud flat or tidal creek, it would be hard to miss these tiny decapods scurrying everywhere. Their single huge claws are a clear giveaway that they are fiddler crabs. Only males have this enlarged pincer. One male's large claw can make up 65 percent of his total body weight! Males wave their pincers to attract females for mating. The back-and-forth waving movement looks like a musician playing a fiddle and gave these crabs their common name. Males also stomp their legs and make noises to attract females.

Areas in which fiddler crabs live are marked with their small burrows. Each individual crab has its own burrow, which is usually about 1/2 inch (1 cm) wide and goes straight down almost 12 inches (30 cm) into the mud. These burrows give fiddler crabs a safe place to hide during high tide and to escape from predators. At low tide, the burrows are filled with water, which keeps the crabs nice and wet.

Fiddler crabs eat tiny particles of plant and animal matter in the sand and mud. A crab first scrapes the surface sediment up into its claws and then transfers the sediment to its mouth. Fiddler crabs have complex mouth systems that filter the nutrients out of the sand.

Once the crab is finished with a mouthful, it spits out a small pellet of clean sand.

Male fiddler crabs cannot use their large pincers for feeding because they are too big. Because they only have one small feeding claw, they can only get half as much food at a time. So they have to spend twice as much time feeding as do female fiddler crabs.

Shrimps

FAMILY: Padalidae
COMMON EXAMPLE: Northern shrimp
GENUS AND SPECIES: *Pandalus borealis*
SIZE: about 5 to 7 inches (12 to 17 cm)

Northern shrimps can be found in both the Atlantic and Pacific Oceans. In the Atlantic, they inhabit the colder northern waters from Greenland to the northern United States, Iceland, and northern Great Britain. In Pacific waters, they are found from Japan to the Bering Sea. Many Canadian fisheries specialize in catching northern shrimps for sale throughout the world.

Like most other shrimp species, northern shrimps are great swimmers. These shrimps have strong appendages, called pleopods, on their tails that act like paddles. The shrimps use their pleopods to move quickly through the chilly water. They need to move fast because they are food for many species of ocean animals, including halibut, cod, and seals.

Northern shrimps share another trait with some of their other shrimp cousins: They are hermaphrodites, which means they have the reproductive organs of both sexes. Young shrimps start life as males and usually remain males for about three years. In the fourth year, the shrimps' male organs are replaced by female reproductive organs, and the shrimps spend the rest of their lives as females.

After mating, a female might carry as many as 1,700 fertilized eggs. When the eggs hatch into larvae, they float to the surface to feed on tiny water organisms. They molt several times, casting off their old outer shells.

Crabs

FAMILY: Portunidae
COMMON EXAMPLE: European green crab
GENUS AND SPECIES: *Carcinus maenas*
SIZE: 2 1/2 to 4 inches (6 to 10 cm)

In spite of its name, the European green crab isn't always green. Its top shell is often dark brown to dark green, with small yellow patches. There is even a red-colored European green crab. The undersides of most European green crabs can also be quite colorful, changing from green to orange to red during the molting cycle.

This decapod's native home is the Atlantic coast of Europe and northern Africa. European green crabs live in a wide variety of habitats, including rocky shores, beaches, tidal marshes, and sand flats. They also can live in a wide range of ocean temperatures, which gives them an edge on survival in many areas.

In Europe, the European green crab isn't a welcome native. It is a greedy eater and a strong, aggressive predator, attacking other shellfish populations such as mussels, clams, and oysters. Unlike many other crab species, the European green crab is capable of learning new behaviors, such as better ways to hunt and kill. This makes it especially dangerous to its prey.

During the last century, this unwelcome decapod has become a world traveler, invading waters far beyond its native range. European green crabs can now be found in South Africa, Australia,

Japan, and on both North American coasts. The adaptability of this **invader species** to different habitats means that it has thrived in its new homes, threatening shellfish fisheries worldwide.

Lobsters

FAMILY: *Scyllaridae*

COMMON EXAMPLE: Hawaiian slipper lobster, ula pehu

GENUS AND SPECIES: *Scyllarides squammosus*

SIZE: from 7 to 19 inches (18 to 50 cm)

Hawaiian slipper lobsters look nothing like their American counterparts. The flat body of a slipper lobster has two shovel-like appendages on the head, but they are not for digging. They are really the lobster's antennae. They don't have the distinctive large pincers that most other lobsters boast.

Slipper lobsters live in the caves and crevices of coral reefs and other ocean formations in the Pacific Ocean. Their flat bodies come in very handy during the day, when they hide by clinging tightly to rock walls and cave roofs. Their plain coloration helps them blend in with their rocky surroundings. At night, the lobsters forage slowly along the rocks and reefs, looking for prey such as snails, oysters, sea anemones, fishes, and other lobsters. They will also feast on dead animal matter if they find it.

Summertime is mating season for slipper lobsters. Males fertilize the females' eggs by attaching sticky sperm packets to the females' abdomens. The females carry packets of fertilized eggs, cleaning them with a special set of claws on their last pair of walking legs. As the eggs mature, they begin to resemble red or black

berries. Because of this unusual trait, egg-carrying females are often called "berried" females.

The Hawaiian slipper lobster population is not large enough to be fished for food, so it is not likely that you'll see one of these bumpy lobsters on your dinner plate anytime soon.

Lobsters

FAMILY: Palinuridae
COMMON EXAMPLE: Caribbean spiny lobster
GENUS AND SPECIES: *Panulirus argus*
SIZE: 24 inches (60 cm)

The first thing you notice about the Caribbean spiny lobster is the way it got its name—from the two large antennae and the spines that stick out all over its body. The second thing that's unusual about this decapod is that it doesn't have the familiar large front pincers that other lobsters have. Because this lobster lacks these defensive pincers, it needs the spines for protection against predators.

The Caribbean spiny lobster lives in warm-water areas of the Atlantic Ocean, such as near the Caribbean islands. It spends most of the daylight hours hiding in cracks and crevices in rocks and on the ocean floor. At night, however, it sets out along the ocean floor in search of a meal. Like other lobsters, the Caribbean spiny lobster eats animal and plant material, **scavenging** dead matter from the sea floor and hunting smaller fishes, mollusks, and other crustaceans.

Each fall, Caribbean spiny lobsters get the urge to travel. Scientists aren't sure why the lobsters go on the move, but they suspect it could be because of the temperature drop or the change in the length of daylight. Slowly, every spiny lobster in an area will march away, crawling slowly in a long straight line that can sometimes include more than sixty lobsters. Thousands of spiny lobsters will find a line

and join in the mass migration. They travel south nonstop, day and night, staying in a single-file line by putting their antennae on the lobster in front of them. Some lobster lines travel more than 9 miles (14.5 kilometers) a day, not stopping until they are more than 40 miles (64 km) away from where they started.

Shrimps

FAMILY: Stenopodidae
COMMON EXAMPLE: Golden coral shrimp
GENUS AND SPECIES: *Stenopus scutellatus*
SIZE: 1 1/2 to 2 inches (3 to 5 cm)

Divers who visit the Bahamas and other Caribbean islands delight in glimpsing these rare, beautiful shrimps, which live among the sponges and coral reefs from the Gulf of Mexico to Brazil. These shrimps are also popular home aquarium residents because of their bright colors.

Golden coral shrimps—also known as cleaner shrimps—form pairs that live together in quiet, protected holes in reefs for long periods of time. When they get hungry, they don't even leave their holes. Instead, they whip their light-colored **antennae** in the sunny water to attract nearby fishes. When a fish approaches, the golden coral shrimps gently pick parasites and dead tissue from the fish, and nibble on any stray plant matter they can find—without ever leaving their cozy homes.

Cleaner shrimps, such as the golden coral shrimp, are vitally important to the life of a tropical coral reef. They have a good deal going with the other reef fishes: the fishes get a good cleaning, and the shrimps get a good meal. If cleaner shrimps leave a section of coral reef, the area is soon abandoned by all the other reef fishes. When cleaner shrimps are in residence, fishes and other marine life

will sometimes wait patiently in line for their turn under cleaner shrimps' gentle touch. Even large marine animals such as turtles travel to the reefs for this specialty service. Sometimes, fishes that are normally camouflaged will turn pale while they're being groomed by cleaner shrimps, so that the shrimps can pick off the pests more easily.

Shrimps

FAMILY: Hippolytidae
COMMON EXAMPLE: Fiji red cave prawn
GENUS AND SPECIES: *Parhippolyte uveae*
SIZE: 1 inch (2.5 cm)

The Fiji red cave **prawn** enjoys a respect that few other shrimps can boast. For many years, the people of Fiji have considered the red cave prawn to be sacred. Some think that the prawn became revered because of its bright red color. Local superstition holds that bothering or removing a red cave prawn from its home will cause shipwrecks or even death to anyone who dares to disturb the sacred animal.

Fiji red cave prawns can be found in only two locations throughout the Fiji Islands in the Pacific Ocean: the island of Vatulele and Naweni village on the island of Vanua Levu. In both places, the prawns live in a unique habitat: lava rock pools near the sea that are filled with salty water. Local villagers still need permission from the village chief to visit the pools and pay their respects to the sacred decapods.

Aside from its status as a famous Fiji resident, the red cave prawn is very much like its shrimp cousins all over the Pacific. It is a good swimmer, using its strong tail to swim forward by paddling or to move backward by stroking swiftly.

Recently, the government of Fiji made the red cave prawn even more famous by putting it on a postage stamp. Now this tiny, rare

decapod, found in only two places on Earth, can travel by letter and
postcard all over the world.

Crabs

FAMILY: Grapsidae
COMMON EXAMPLE: Chinese mitten crab
GENUS AND SPECIES: *Eriocheir sinensis*
SIZE: 2 to 4 inches (5 to 10 cm)

One look at this crab and it's easy to see where it got part of its name. The "mittens" on its claws aren't cold-weather wear, but dense patches of hair. The "Chinese" part of its name comes from the area that was this decapod's original home: the Yellow Sea region of Korea and China. Today, however, the Chinese mitten crab enjoys a worldwide existence. It can be found in Europe and parts of the United States as a troublesome invader.

Mitten crabs spend most of their lives in freshwater such as rivers. By the time the crabs are four or five years old, they begin their long migration downstream to mate. After mating, the females spend the winter in deep ocean water, returning to their freshwater habitats in the spring to lay their eggs.

The Chinese mitten crab is a hearty decapod that can withstand many different habitats and weather conditions. This gives it the edge as an invader species, because it can survive in places far outside its native habitat. Mitten crabs eat both plants and animals and have been known to devour smaller decapods, worms, and clams. They also love stealing bait from fishermen, making them a big nuisance.

Very little can stop a Chinese mitten crab when it is on the move. If it is blocked by a dam or other barrier during its migration, it will leave the water and walk around the obstacle! Chinese mitten crabs have been found on roads, airport runways, parking lots, yards, and swimming pools.

History of Lobstering

Of all the decapods, the lobster is the best known. Huge fishing industries have grown up around lobsters, and they have become a multimillion-dollar business for lobster fishermen. Today, lobsters are considered to be a somewhat rare delicacy, commanding high prices in seafood markets and expensive restaurants. But lobsters haven't always enjoyed such high-class status.

Long ago, when Native American tribes lived freely in the northeastern region of the United States, lobsters were so common that they were used as fertilizer for fields. Native Americans also used lobster meat as bait to catch other fish. When European colonists arrived, they considered lobsters to be food for the poor because they were so plentiful that even the poorest person could catch and eat them. At that time, lobsters were caught in tidal pools and fed to children and prisoners. Indentured servants—people who received passage to the New World in exchange for service for a specified time—rebelled against being served lobster all the time. Some made sure that their service contracts stated that they wouldn't have to eat lobster more than three times a week.

The waters off the New England coast were once so filled with lobsters that people could simply gather them by hand along the shoreline. Until the early 1800s, that was how all lobsters were harvested. Around 1850, fishermen in Maine got the bright idea to use lobster traps, and eventually trapping became the common form

A fisherman removes an American lobster from a trap.

of lobster fishing. Today, Maine is the largest lobster-producing state in the United States. In 2000, more than 57 million pounds of lobsters were caught. That was more than twice the amount of any lobster catch in the last 30 years. Most of them are destined for stores and restaurants in the United States, although many are shipped to other countries. Each year Maine issues about 7,000 licenses for lobster harvesting.

To avoid the dangers of overfishing, there are strict limits on the size of the lobsters that fishermen can catch. The minimum legal size for a lobster is 3.25 inches (8.25 cm), from the eye socket to the beginning of the tail. That is known as

A fisherman measures the lobster to make sure it is large enough to keep.

the carapace. A lobster this size weighs about half a pound (0.2 kg). Also, females carrying eggs, regardless of size, must be released. Some environmentally conscious lobster fishermen cut a small, V-shaped notch in the tail of any female before letting it go. This tells other lobster fishermen that this lobster should not be harvested. Instead, she will stay in the water to breed for many years to come.

Maine also has a maximum size for the lobsters that can be caught—those with a 5-inch (12.7-cm) carapace length. This ensures that the biggest lobsters and therefore the biggest breeders (which might carry more than 100,000 eggs each) will remain alive to sustain the lobster population.

Lobstermen sometimes find surprises when they haul in their catches. In 1977, a fisherman in the Northeast caught a lobster that weighed almost 45 pounds (20 kg). It measured 3 1/2 feet (1 m) long from its tail to the end of its claw. To this day it remains the largest crustacean ever caught.

Words to Know

antennae—one of a pair of slender moveable sensory organs on the head of decapods

chelipeds—large, heavy pincers

class—a group of creatures within a phylum that share certain characteristics

crustaceans—members of a class of mostly aquatic arthropods that have a hard exoskeleton

estuary—the area of water where a river meets the ocean

family—a group of creatures within an order that share certain characteristics

genus (plural **genera**)—a group of creatures within a family that share certain characteristics

invader species—a creature that invades a habitat that is not its native habitat

habitat—the natural environment of an animal or plant

kingdom—the most general group of biological classification

larvae—immature, early stage of a decapod

molt—to shed or cast off an outer layer of skin, hair, or shell

order—creatures within a class that share certain characteristics

parasite—a creature that lives in, on, or with another creature

prawn—a type of shrimp

predacious—an animal that will catch and eat any other animal that is the right size and is available

predator—an animal that hunts other animals for food

scavenge—to feed on dead animal and plant matter

spawn—to produce young in large numbers

species—a group of creatures within a genus that share certain characteristics. Members of a species can mate and produce young.

thorax—the middle section of a decapod's body

Learning More

Books

Fowler, Allan. *Shellfish Aren't Fish*. Danbury, CT: Children's Press, 1999.

Greenway, Theresa. *The Secret World of Crabs*. Austin, TX: Raintree/Steck Vaughn, 2001.

Rotman, Jeffrey L. *Lobsters: Gangsters of the Sea*. New York: Cobblehill Books, 1994.

Tibbits, Christiane. *Seashells, Crabs and Sea Stars*. Minocqua, WI: Northword Press, 1999.

On Line Sites

Lobsters
http://www.abc-kid.com/lobster/

Crustaceans
http://wwwlk12.hi.us/~hapunaha/crustaceans.htm

All About Maine Wildlife: Lobsters
http://www.state.me.us/sos/kids/allabout/wildlife/lobster.htm

Index

About the Author

Allison Lassieur has written more than 40 books about history, science, animals, cultures, and health. She lives with her husband Chuck and their two cats in a 100-year-old house in Pennsylvania.